D0772789

WITHDRAWN

Extreme
Motorcycle Racing

Clive Gifford

Capstone press

Fact Finders is published by Capstone Press,
a Capstone Publishers company.
151 Good Counsel Drive, P.O. Box 669,
Mankato, Minnesota 56002.
www.capstonepress.com

Produced for A & C Black by
MONKEY PUZZLE MEDIA Ltd   Monkey Puzzle Media Ltd
48 York Avenue
Hove BN3 1PJ, UK

First published 2009
Copyright © 2009 A & C Black Publishers Limited

No part of this publication may be reproduced in whole
or in part, or stored in a retrieval system, or transmitted
in any form or by any means, electronic, mechanical,
photocopying, recording, or otherwise, without written
permission of the publisher.
For information regarding permission, write to Capstone
Press, 151 Good Counsel Drive, P.O. Box 669, Dept. R,
Mankato, Minnesota 56002.

The right of Clive Gifford to be identified as the author of
this Work has been asserted by him in accordance with
the Copyright, Designs and Patents Act 1988.

Library of Congress Cataloging-in-Publication Data

Gifford, Clive.
   Extreme motorcycle racing / By Clive Gifford.
   p. cm. -- (Fact finders. extreme adventures!)
   Includes bibliographical references and index.
   Summary: "Describes the most extreme types of
   motorcycle races and events, including MotoGP,
   motocross, land speed racing, ice speedway, and
   top-fuel motorcycle drag racing"--Provided by publisher.
   ISBN 978-1-4296-4556-0 (library binding)
   ISBN 978-1-4296-4615-4 (pbk.)
1. Motorcycle racing--Juvenile literature. 2. Motocross--
Juvenile literature. 3. Drag racing--Juvenile literature.
I. Title. II. Series.

GV1060.G53 2010
796.7'5--dc22

2009028513

Editor: Susie Brooks
Design: Mayer Media Ltd
Picture research: Lynda Lines
Series consultants: Jane Turner and James de Winter

This book is produced using paper that is made from
wood grown in managed, sustainable forests. It is natural,
renewable, and recyclable. The logging and manufacturing
processes conform to the environmental regulations of the
country of origin.

Printed in Malaysia by Tien Wah Press (Pte.) Ltd

102009
005558

Picture acknowledgements
Action Images pp. 1 (Reuters/John Pryke), 11 (Reuters/
Michael Kooren), 14 (Steven Paston), 16 (Sporting
Pictures), 16–17 (Sporting Pictures), 18 (MSI), 19 (Reuters/
John Pryke); Action Plus p. 13 (Leo Mason); A2 Wind
Tunnel LLC p. 10; Corbis pp. 6 (Patrick Bennett), 8 (John
W. Gertz/zefa), 9 (Leah Warkentin/Design Pics), 22
(Lefevre/ASA/epa), 25 (Jens Wolf/epa); Getty Images
pp. 5, 7 (Bongarts), 15 (Mario Laporta/AFP), 20 (Pascal
Rondeau/ Allsport), 20–21 (Mike Cooper/Allsport),
23 (Digital Vision), 24 (Volker Hartmann/AFP), 26
(Raveendran/AFP), 27 (Tony Ashby/AFP); MPM Images
p. 28; New Zealand MiniMoto Race Club p. 4; Rocky-
Robinson.com p. 29; Zodiac Drag Race Team p. 12
(Stefan Boman).

The front cover shows MotoGP drivers Nicky Hayden
and Loris Capirossi at the Indianapolis Motor Speedway
in Indiana (Corbis/Tannen Maury/epa).

Every effort has been made to contact copyright holders
of material reproduced in this book. Any omissions will
be rectified in subsequent printings if notice is given to the
publishers.

CONTENTS

Abbreviations **km** stands for kilometers • **m** stands for meters • **ft** stands for feet • **km/h** stands for kilometers per hour • **mph** stands for miles per hour

Extreme machines

Imagine riding a motorcycle that's twice as fast as your family's car—maybe even faster! Roaring beneath you is a power-packed engine that can whizz you up to top speed in seconds. Hold on tight!

The Suzuki Hayabusa is one of the fastest, meanest machines around. It's a superfast bike, with a big engine creating enormous power. Its top speed is limited by law to 185 miles per hour (297 kilometers per hour)—but it can go faster!

In 2008, Trillium Muir became the world's fastest woman on a bike. Her Hayabusa reached almost 238 miles per hour (383 kilometers per hour). You have to be an expert rider to handle that sort of awesome power.

Even these tiny pocket bikes can reach around 56 mph (90 km/h)!

accelerate to increase speed

Vrmm, vrmm

The Hayabusa engine is so powerful that it has been used as the engine in a sports car—the Westfield Megabusa.

*A Suzuki Hayabusa can **accelerate** from 0 to 62.5 mph (100 km/h) in just 2.7 seconds!*

Tire spins on road surface, causing **friction**.

Powerful engine drives the rear wheel around.

Friction produces heat—and lots of smoke!

Wheel spins.

friction the force that slows movement between two objects rubbing together

Start your engines

When you ride a motorcycle, you're riding a kind of bomb! Explosions are going off many times a second inside a motorcycle engine.

Twist and burn

Riders change their bike's speed using the **throttle**. This is usually a twist grip on the handlebar. It controls how much air is let into the engine's cylinders.

A motorcycle engine has one or more **cylinders**. A precise amount of fuel and air are let into each cylinder. All it needs is a spark to make the mixture explode. This comes from an electrical part called a spark plug.

The explosion pushes a rod called a piston along the cylinder. This movement provides the energy to turn the bike's rear wheel around.

The rider's-eye view: the top dial shows the bike's speed. The bottom dial is a rev counter, which shows how hard the engine is working.

cylinder a tube in an engine where the power is created

Waste gases blast out of the exhaust pipe.

ZOOOM!

Forward twist = slow down.

Right hand controls the throttle.

Back twist = faster.

Six racers speed away on their dirt bikes.

throttle a device for controlling speed

Fuel and air burn in the engine.

Wheelies!

Some riders reckon that two wheels are one too many. They use the power of the engine to lift the bike's front wheel off the ground. It's called "pulling a wheelie."

When you start a motorcycle normally, both tires grip the ground and the bike moves forward on two wheels. But if the amount of power is suddenly increased, the rear wheel thrusts ahead and the front wheel rears up in the air. This is a wheelie.

Careful . . .that rear wheel is digging itself deeper into the desert!

The rider ends a wheelie by decreasing power, which shifts the bike's weight back over the front wheel. Then it's up to **gravity** to pull the wheel to the ground.

Wheeeeeelie!

In 1984, Doug Domokos kept a wheelie going for a staggering 144 miles (232 kilometers).

gravity a force that attracts objects to each other

Too much lean or power, and it's crash time!

Front wheel lifts.

Bike moves forward.

Wheel turns.

Tire grips the ground.

This looks like wheelie good fun—but don't try it at home!

The world's fastest race bikes

The biggest, baddest race bikes of all are MotoGP machines. No expense is spared on these amazing two-wheeled rocket ships.

A MotoGP bike can travel so fast, it's a wonder the wind doesn't knock the rider's head off! MotoGP racers have to tuck themselves out of the wind, or they wouldn't be able to hold on to the handlebars.

MotoGP bikes are designed to slice through the air as smoothly as possible. The bikes are made narrow, with parts tucked in. The rider "tucks in" too, hunched over the fuel tank.

Record racer

During the 2008 Shanghai Grand Prix MotoGP race, Casey Stoner's Ducati reached a record speed of 215.62 miles per hour (347 kilometers per hour).

A race bike is tested in a wind tunnel. Giant fans blast air over the motorcycle, as if it is moving fast.

streamlined shaped so that air flows easily over it

This bike is **streamlined** to cut through the air as smoothly as possible.

Narrow handlebars keep the rider's hands and arms tucked in.

Rider tucks behind the **fairing**.

AIR FLOW

Engine is hidden behind the fairing.

Fairing smooths the air flow around the bike.

fairing a covering that protects from wind and helps with streamlining

Six-second sizzlers

MotoGP not fast enough for you? Try riding a top-fuel drag bike—it feels like having your arms pulled from their sockets!

Pairs of drag bikes race each other along a short, straight piece of track called a drag strip. Don't blink if you're watching—the race will be over in just 6 seconds!

Drag bikes are fitted with incredibly powerful engines. Their top speed is over 217 miles per hour (350 kilometers per hour). Keeping control is a tough task. A long arm called a wheelie bar is fitted to the back of the bike to stop it from doing a massive wheelie.

A drag bike spins its rear wheel before racing. "Burnouts" like this heat the back tire, giving it more grip.

Gas guzzlers

Top-fuel bikes use a fuel called nitromethane instead of gasoline. They use a lot—in fact, 10.5 gallons (40 liters) per kilometer raced!

drag bike a fast motorcycle raced on a short, straight track

The front wheel rears up as the drag bike roars off the starting line.

"Christmas-tree lights" signal the start of the race.

Rider lies flat to avoid being thrown off.

Wheelie bar helps stop the front wheel from lifting too high.

0–100 mph (0–160 km/h) in 1.1 seconds!

Cornering kings

Top bike racers can take corners faster than most people drive in a straight line! How on Earth do their tires grip the track?

The tires grip because they are made of special soft rubber. The weight of the bike and rider pushes the tire against the track surface. A force called friction allows the tire to take hold. Imagine a motorcycle tire made of something slippery, like glass. It wouldn't work very well!

Speedway bikes have no brakes! Riders use the throttle to get the back of the bike to drift sideways through the turn.

Touch down

Only a small part of each tire touches the ground at one time. This is called the contact patch. Incredibly, the contact patch for each tire is no bigger than a credit card.

speedway racing on an oval-shaped dirt track

Valentino Rossi leads a race through a pair of turns. Mid-turn, the riders' knees skim the ground—or even scrape it.

PADDING! Knee slider glides above or scrapes the track surface.

Leaning the bike forces it to turn.

Bike wants to go straight.

2 LEAN!

1 VROOM!

FRICTION! Tires grip the track.

Gripping stuff

Protective guard stops the wheel from spiking other riders.

Ouch! Ninety sharp steel spikes are on the front wheel. The rear has 200–500!

Motorcycles on ice? No kidding. Ice speedway is a serious sport with its own World Championships. The secret is in the special tires, which provide grip on the most slippery of surfaces.

Ice speedway bikes race around short, oval tracks. They have just enough fuel in their tiny tanks for four laps of the track. But there's nothing else puny about these machines!

The bikes reach 81 miles per hour (130 kilometers per hour) on the short straights, and barely slow down for each tight, icy bend. The spikes on their wheels dig into the ice, which produces the grip needed to race on ice.

Baling out

If they lose it, ice speedway riders hit a piled-up snowbank or straw bales on the outside edge of the track.

Spikes dig in for extreme grip.

Speed around bend = 56–62 mph (90–100 km/h)

GRIP

SPEED

Ice speedway riders take every corner with extreme lean.
Their knees and handlebars just brush the ice!

CRASH!

Most of the time, grip (or friction) is a rider's friend, keeping the tires steady. But once in a while, grip goes wrong and turns out to be a rider's enemy . . .

These riders are performing a "stoppie." Using the front brake hard stops the front wheel, but the back wheel keeps moving and lifts up!

Air bag

The Honda Goldwing GL1800 has an **air bag** to protect a rider's head. In a head-on crash, the bag inflates in 0.06 seconds.

One of the most spectacular crashes you can have is a "highside." This happens when the rear tire loses grip in a corner. The back of the bike starts to slide sideways. It's embarrassing, but not disastrous—unless the back tire grips the track again. The bike suddenly stops sliding and falls over, flinging the rider into the air.

air bag an inflatable cushion that protects a driver in a crash

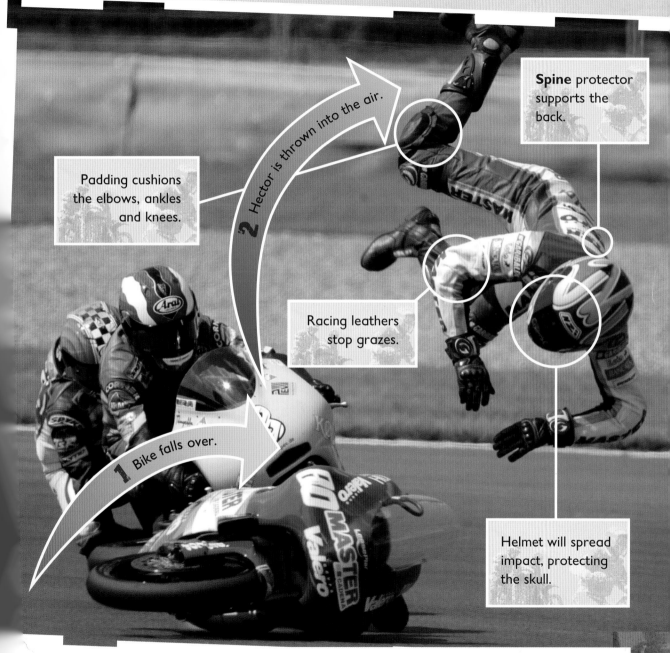

Sixteen-year-old Hector Barbera flies through the air at the 2002 British 125cc Grand Prix. He walked away from this crash and won the race the next year.

Spine protector supports the back.

Padding cushions the elbows, ankles and knees.

2 Hector is thrown into the air.

Racing leathers stop grazes.

1 Bike falls over.

Helmet will spread impact, protecting the skull.

spine the backbone

Sidecar racer

Passengers on extreme sidecar race bikes don't just sit there. They're expected to help the driver by leaning out over the track, skimming its surface!

Weight over the back wheel = more grip = more speed!

Sidecar passengers are known as "monkeys," for the way they scramble all over the vehicle. They do this because sidecars don't lean into turns like regular motorcycles. Instead, they enter the turn upright, and the monkey shifts his or her body weight to keep the sidecar from flipping up. When there is a series of left and right turns, a monkey has to move fast!

Sidecar star

Steve Webster is the most successful sidecar racer ever. He has won ten Sidecar World Championships. In 181 races, he finished in the top three 131 times.

sidecar a one-wheeled attachment to a bike, allowing a passenger

A sidecar enters a left turn at the famous Nürburgring *track* in Germany.

Passenger's weight balances the lifting wheel and keeps the sidecar level.

Can I have a seat next time?

Sidecar wants to lift.

Body weight pulls down.

Rough riders

Motorcycles are not just ridden at extreme speeds. They are ridden in extreme places, too. Welcome to the world of the rough riders—where bumps, jumps, and dirt are guaranteed.

Off-road riding is a dangerous sport. Broken bones are common, and even top riders sometimes have to miss races because they are injured. The best racer ever, Ricky Carmichael, had to sit out the whole 2005 **Supercross** season because he was injured.

To help with rocky rides, off-road bikes need good **suspension**. This lessens the shock of the impact when a bike goes over a bump or lands from a jump.

Over 1,000 rough riders tackle the crazy Enduro du Touquet race. The race is 10 miles (16 km) long over massive sand dunes.

GOAT

Ricky Carmichael's nickname was **GOAT** (Greatest Of All Time)! In 2002, he recorded the first-ever "perfect season"—a race season in which he was unbeaten in any race. Then he did it again in 2004!

Supercross off-road racing using specialized, high-performance bikes

Motocross riders nail a jump.

Suspension up
softens landing.

BOING!

Front fork telescopes
in and then out to
absorb impact.

Bike powers away
so it doesn't get
bogged down.

THROTTLE ON!

suspension a system of shock absorbers designed to reduce bumps

BIG beasts

Some bikes are big—really BIG! The biggest factory-produced motorcycles weigh about six times as much as an average man. But some one-off machines are much larger.

Tall order

Dream Big took Gregory Dunham three years to build. The enormous handlebars are just for show. The real steering is done using a car steering wheel!

Designers normally try to keep the weight of their motorcycles low. Less weight helps a bike move faster and use less fuel. But Tilo Niebel wasn't worried about weight when he built the *Harzer Bike Schmiede*.

With a height of 11.25 ft (3.429 m), Dream Big is the world's tallest motorcycle.

Harzer Bike Schmiede is the world's heaviest motorcycle-sidecar. It weighs 5.25 tons (4.7 metric tons)—more than twenty-one Suzuki Hayabusas!

The *Harzer Bike Schmiede*'s *engine* comes from a Russian T55 tank and has twelve cylinders—six times as many as some bikes!

Almost 10 ft (3 m) wide

Russian tank badge

Old searchlight as front headlight

Over 16 ft (5 m) long

Sidecar is built from the front of an old Russian truck.

Tires are over 3 ft (1 m) tall.

Biking on air

Most bikers are happy to stay in their seats. But there's one breed of biker that thinks a ride spent seated is a dull one indeed—the freestyle motocross rider!

Freestyle motocross is often called FMX. The riders launch their bikes way up into the air, high enough to jump through a first-floor window. Not content with daredevil leaps, they started inventing crazy tricks in midair, including:

- **Backflip** (single or double)— bike and rider do one or two full backward rotations.
- **Can can**—rider lifts a foot over the seat and back again.
- **Superman seatgrab**—rider gets off the bike in midair, holding on only to the seat, legs sticking straight out behind.

Thirteen on a single bike—surely that's against the law? These men should know—they're all from the Indian police!

WEIGHT

WEIGHT

Weight has to be evenly balanced.

Daredevil Robbie Maddison momentarily lets go of his bike in midair during the Gravity Games in Perth, Australia.

Rider and bike move at the same speed.

As long as the rider doesn't push the bike away from him, it's safe to let go.

Bike moves through the air.

Big air

Australian stunt rider Robbie Maddison gained REALLY big air in 2008. His world motorcycle jump record was a whopping 351 feet (106.98 meters).

Record breakers

This is it, the ultimate test of motorcycle muscle—the World Motorcycle Land Speed Record. Since 2006, it's been a head-to-head battle between two monstrous machines.

Round One went to Rocky Robinson riding the *Top 1 Oil Ack Attack*. In September 2006, it reached a staggering 342.8 miles per hour (551.7 kilometers per hour). Two days later, Chris Carr on the *Bub Lucky 7* topped it with 350.9 miles per hour (564.7 kilometers per hour). Ouch!

Rocky and his team licked their wounds and tried again in 2008. The end result: 360.9 miles per hour (580.8 kilometers per hour). Now that's *extreme!*

In 1907, Glenn Curtiss built his own bike with no brakes and reached 136 mph (219 km/h). No motorcycle would go faster until 1930.

Blind Ninja

In 2003, Billy Baxter created a new blind world speed record of 164.9 miles per hour (265.38 kilometers per hour), riding a Kawasaki Ninja while wearing a blindfold.

We hold the world record!

Not for much longer . . .

TWO Suzuki Hayabusa engines provide power.

Rocky sat here.

Stabilizer wheel supports the bike when standing still.

Wheel pops back behind the panel for racing.

Skin made of **carbon fiber**.

The Bub Lucky 7 (back) and Top 1 Oil Ack Attack line up on Bonneville Salt Flats, ready for record-breaking extreme-speed action.

carbon fiber a lightweight but very strong material

Glossary

accelerate to increase speed

air bag an inflatable cushion that protects a driver in a crash

carbon fiber a lightweight but very strong material

cylinder a tube in an engine where the power is created

drag bike a fast motorcycle raced on a short, straight track

fairing a covering that protects from wind and helps with streamlining

friction the force that slows movement between two objects rubbing together

gravity a force that attracts objects to each other

sidecar a one-wheeled attachment to a bike, allowing a passenger

speedway racing on an oval-shaped dirt track

spine the backbone

streamlined shaped so that air flows easily over it

Supercross off-road racing using specialized, high-performance bikes

suspension a system of shock absorbers designed to reduce bumps

throttle a device for controlling speed

Further information

Books

The Illustrated Encyclopedia of Motorcycles by Roland Brown (Southwater, 2007) Learn all about more than 200 makes of bikes in this photo-packed book.

Motorbikes by Chris Oxlade (Heinemann Library, 2008) Lots of information on some of the biggest and fastest motorcycles around.

Motocross by Paul Mason (Hodder Children's Books, 2001) All you need to know about the extreme sport of motocross.

The Need For Speed: Motorbikes by Philip Raby & Simon Nix (Lerner, 1999) Found in libraries and on the Internet, a great book on extreme motorcycles and races.

Magazines

There are dozens of motorcycle magazines out there covering every type of motorcycle. In the United States, ***Cycle World***, ***Roadracing World*** and ***Dirt Rider*** are popular while ***Transworld Motocross*** is the biggest motocross mag on the planet. In the UK, ***Bike*** and the newspaper ***MCN*** are both popular, while ***Motorcycle Racer*** is great for road and track racing. Top Australian magazines include ***Two Wheels***, ***Heavy Duty*** and ***ADB*** (***Australasian Dirt Bike***).

Web sites

FactHound offers a safe, fun way to find Internet sites related to this book. All of the sites on FactHound have been researched by our staff. Visit *www.facthound.com* for age-appropriate sites. You may browse subjects by clicking on letters, or by clicking on pictures and words. **FactHound will fetch the best sites for you!**

Film

Faster directed by Mark Neale (Dorna Sports, 2003) Narrated by motorcycle-mad actor, Ewan McGregor, this exciting documentary tells the story of the MotoGP championship.

Index

31901047100732